*V*isiting the *P*ast

Fort Laramie

Tristan Boyer Binns

Heinemann Library
Chicago, Illinois

Designed by Wilkinson Design
Photographs by Tristan Boyer Binns
Illustrations by David Westerfield
Printed and bound at Lake Book, Chicago, Illinois, U.S.A.

06 05 04 03 02
10 9 8 7 6 5 4 3 2 1

Library of Congress Cataloging-In-Publication Data
Binns, Tristan Boyer, 1968-
  Fort Laramie / Tristan Boyer Binns.
      p. cm. -- (Visiting the past)
Includes bibliographical references and index.
  ISBN 1-58810-271-8 (lib. bdg.)   ISBN 1-58810-409-5 (pbk. bdg.)
  1. Fort Laramie (Wyo.)--History--Juvenile literature. 2. Frontier and
pioneer life--Wyoming--Fort Laramie--Juvenile literature. [1. Fort
Laramie (Wyo.) 2. Frontier and pioneer life--Wyoming--Fort Laramie.] I.
Title. II. Series.
  F769.F6 B56 2001
  978.7'18--dc21
                          2001000841

Acknowledgments
The author and publishers would like to thank the following for permission to reproduce photographs
State Historical Society, p. 9a; The Newberry Library, Chicago, p. 12b;

The author and publishers would like to thank Sherry Linesbury and Louise Sampson at Fort Laramie
National Historic Site and Barbara Agresti.

Special thanks to Tammy Benson and Rex Norman at Fort Laramie National Historic Site for their
expertise in the preparation of this book as well as for their interest and enthusiasm in the project.

Some words in the book appear in bold, **like this.**
You can find out what they mean by looking in the glossary.

Contents

The Western Lands

In 1803, the United States was less than half the size it is now. President Thomas Jefferson made the **Louisiana Purchase** and doubled the amount of land in the country. This new land stretched from the Mississippi River west to the Rocky Mountains, and few white people had ever seen it. Jefferson sent Meriwether Lewis and William Clark to explore and record what they saw as they traveled west through land inhabited by millions of Native Americans. When they returned in 1806, people were eager to hear about their discoveries. Many were already thinking about moving west.

In the 1820s, a few white men adopted the Native American ways of life and moved to the lands west of the Mississippi River. They made a living trapping and selling beaver furs. Businessmen from the East built small forts at well-traveled places throughout the West, in present-day states like Colorado, Wyoming, and Montana.

The **Plains** tribes of Native Americans and the few white people who lived in the West got along. There were not many white men willing to live the hard life that the western **frontier** demanded. However, this changed when the first wagon train traveled on what became the Oregon Trail in 1841. Soon, thousands of families passed through the western lands heading for Utah, California, and Oregon. These people thought they had the right to pass through and settle on land on which the Plains tribes had lived for generations.

In the 1840s, as the number of **emigrants** increased, troubles between the Native Americans and the white settlers also increased. The U.S. government took over many of the trading forts to use as military bases and to help protect the travelers. It also worked with the Native Americans to solve the problems caused by settlers' movement through and settlement of Native American land.

◀ These traps were used to catch small animals, such as beavers. Traders working at the forts sold traps and often traded them for animal furs.

Soldiers **negotiated** and enforced **treaties** with the Native Americans. These tribes were supposed to leave the settlers alone and give up lands for settlers to farm and ranch. However, white settlers often broke the terms of these treaties, leading to warfare where many people were killed on both sides.

In 1869, the **Transcontinental** Railroad was finished. Settlers moving west could take the train instead of wagons on the Oregon Trail. Then gold was discovered in the **sacred** Native American Black Hills of South Dakota in 1874. Warfare began again between the Native Americans and the white people. By 1877, the wars were over, and all the Native Americans in the West were moved onto **reservations**. By the end of the century the West was almost entirely settled, and the army closed most of its frontier forts.

▲ Settlers passed through dry and dusty lands. During the summer, these low cactus grow, but during the winter snow will cover them.

▲ Travelers going west passed through areas of soft sandstone, leaving wagon wheel marks behind.

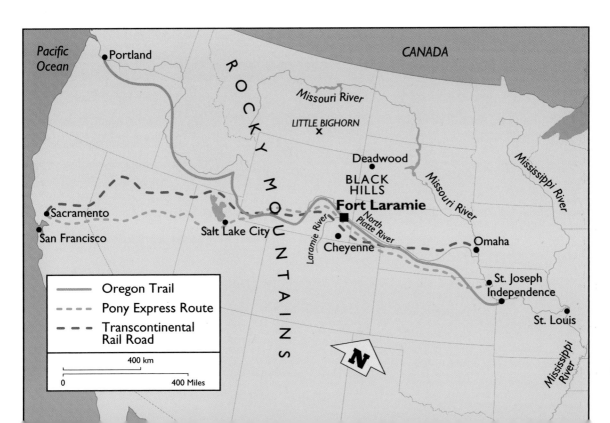

Trappers and Traders

Soon after the first white people explored the West, some of them moved into the Rocky Mountains to live as trappers. To be a successful trapper, or **mountain man**, a man had to adapt to living in this new environment. For many white men, this meant living as the local Native Americans did and also marrying Native American women.

▲ This painting of a Sioux camp at Fort Laramie was made by a Sioux artist.

These "trapping families" spent most of the year trapping beaver and cleaning pelts, or furs. In the 1830s, the demand for beaver pelts went down. Trappers then became hunters and began to trade buffalo hides, called robes. They collected many robes and then traded the robes for goods they couldn't make for themselves. They traded for blankets, beads, tobacco, whiskey, gunpowder, and lead to make bullets.

◀ Built in 1834, Fort William was named after William Sublette, a trapper and businessman. The fort was a meeting place for mountain men, frontier businessmen, and Plains Native Americans. It was the first fort on the site of today's Fort Laramie.

Successful traders were smart businessmen and frontiersmen. They knew how to live and work in the West. They built forts and then sent runners into the hills to tell the local Native Americans and mountain men about their services. Whether trading beaver or buffalo, people could trade several different ways. Native American and white trappers came to the forts with their furs to trade. Some trappers waited to trade at a big annual meeting of trappers and traders, called a *rendezvous*. A rendezvous was a fun time, with dancing and storytelling. Other Native American trappers waited for the winter, when traders would move into the mountains with a limited supply of goods to trade in their own winter villages.

▲ Buffalo robes were pressed into bales using a simple wood press like this.

Most Native Americans and mountain men traded carefully for what they needed. Sometimes white traders would give the Native Americans whiskey, and then make an unfair trade. A fair trade with a Native American family took a long time. They demanded very high quality goods for their robes. The entire family worked to produce the robes, and even a good year only meant about twenty extra robes. Wives did the trading while their husbands stood nearby. Even though the husbands could give their opinions, they usually left the decisions to their wives.

Fort Laramie was a successful trading fort. The fort was needed to store the buffalo robes, which were big and bulky. About 10,000 robes passed through Fort Laramie each year, bundled into bales of 100 robes.

▼ A bale of buffalo robes looked like this white bale, wrapped in rope.

▲ Here are some of the furs traded at Fort Laramie.

Fort Laramie

The North Platte River is wide, slow, shallow, and muddy. It meets the Laramie River, which flows faster and is clearer, at a good place to build a trading fort. It is a lonely site, with no natural protection from the harsh climate, which is often very dry, then muddy, and usually windy. The summer heat reaches over 100°F (38° C), and winter cold plunges to -40°F (–40° C). Fort Laramie was built in that location because it was near the hills where trappers lived and in the heart of traditional Sioux Indian lands.

In 1834, the Rocky Mountain Fur Company built the first wooden fort on the site that is now Fort Laramie.

It was a trading post where **mountain men** and Native Americans brought their furs. Traders at the fort sent runners into the mountains to trade with the trappers there.

This fort, known as Fort William, was sold in 1835 to a group of trappers and again in 1836 to the American Fur Company. It was rebuilt from **adobe** in 1841 near the original site. The new fort was named Fort John, but people started calling it Fort Laramie, after Jacques La Ramie, a French-Canadian trapper. As the fur trade died, settlers began to travel the Oregon Trail, using Fort Laramie as a rest and supply stop.

▼ Today, the Laramie River is lined by trees, mostly cottonwoods. In the 1800s, with no human-built dams along it, yearly floods drowned young trees. Beavers cut down any trees that did grow. As the beavers were trapped, and the river was dammed, trees began to grow along its banks.

◀ Fort John was built on a bluff overlooking the Laramie River. It was named for John Sarpy, a partner in the American Fur Company. Most workers and travelers called it Fort Laramie.

▲ Fort John stood here, between the parade ground and the river.

▲ The magazine held all the ammunition at the fort.

The United States government bought Fort Laramie in 1849. As the army built new buildings, the old adobe decayed and fell into ruin. By 1862, all of old Fort Laramie was gone. The new fort had no outside walls. It looked like a strange collection of buildings made from a number of different materials.

Fort Laramie joined the East with the West by serving as a link in the chain of communication. Overland mail, the **Pony Express,** and the **transcontinental** telegraph all had stops at Fort Laramie.

By the end of the 1860s, the flood of **emigrants** slowed but the fighting with Native Americans picked up. Soldiers from Fort Laramie fought in the wars with the Native Americans. When the wars ended in 1877, Fort Laramie's role changed again. The fort's soldiers protected the new emigrants—**prospectors**—moving to the Black Hills looking for gold. The fort became an important stop on the Cheyenne–Deadwood stagecoach route in present-day South Dakota. In 1890, Fort Laramie was finally closed.

The army's role at Fort Laramie changed over time as the situations and conditions in the West changed. Even after the U.S. Army took over in 1849, the fort was still an important trading post for Native Americans and **mountain men** in the area. The fort trader had a contract with the army to run the trading post and fort store, to supply firewood, and to run the bars and other non-army activities. He was the richest man in the fort and lived in the nicest house.

When the United States government bought Fort Laramie, it looked like a typical **frontier** trading fort. But over time, new buildings were constructed and the original fort was knocked down. Officials planned to build a wall around the new fort buildings. But that was too expensive and there wasn't a great threat to the fort, so the wall was never built.

The heart of a fort is the parade ground. It is a field at the center of the buildings. At Fort Laramie, the parade ground was dirt, which got muddy in the rain and dusty in dry weather. Every day at 9 A.M., the guards on duty changed shifts in a ceremony on the parade ground.

Over the 41 years that Fort Laramie was an army post, there was no plan that outlined what would be built and how it would look. So the new

▲ The most famous building, an officers' quarters called Old Bedlam, looks like it belongs on a southern plantation.

buildings all looked different. Some were **Victorian**-style houses, and others were low, square, and plain. Buildings at Fort Laramie were made from **adobe, lime grout** concrete, or wood. Wood was hauled in from 30 to 50 miles (48 to 81 kilometers) away because few trees grew near the fort.

► In 1875, the army built a much-needed iron bridge over the North Platte River. The army had to protect the land to the north but couldn't get across the river easily. The nearest bridge was in present-day Nebraska, about 50 miles (81 kilometers) away. Once the bridge was built, it allowed stagecoach and freight traffic, too.

People living at Fort Laramie grew into a close community, partly because the nearest town of Cheyenne was 90 miles (145 kilometers) away. In the East, army forts had very separate social lives for officers and **enlisted** men. In the West, the lives of officers and enlisted men crossed much more, mainly because there were so few people on the frontier.

Fort Laramie was a very large operation by the late 1800s. There were soldiers and officers and their families. Laundresses, who lived across the river, were army employees, too. Other craftspeople, like carpenters, blacksmiths, and wheelwrights, worked at the fort. Big stables housed all the horses. Native American scouts and mountain men guides also worked for the army. Officers also employed servants to cook and keep house.

▼ The fort had the feeling of a small town on the plains, with plenty of activity on most days.

Native Americans and Fort Laramie

The Native Americans who lived around the Fort Laramie area were mostly different tribes of Sioux. They lived off the land, hunting and gathering food. They moved around during the summer, following large herds of buffalo. In the winter, they settled in villages and lived off the food they had stored.

Trading forts were not built to drive the Native Americans out of their lands. The Sioux and the traders needed each other in the business of fur trading and in bartering for necessary goods. About 7,000 local Sioux used Fort Laramie as a trading post. But when settlers passed through Sioux lands in the 1840s, some fighting broke out.

Treaties were signed to try to solve the problems between the Native Americans and the United States. The first treaty came after a big council, or meeting, at Fort Laramie in 1851.

More than 10,000 Native Americans went to this council, but only 1 Sioux was allowed to discuss terms with the United States. Since the Sioux lived in separate tribes with different leaders, not all thought they had agreed to the treaty. The Native Americans agreed to let the settlers move through their lands in return for a payment of $50,000 a year for 50 years. The U.S. government had planned to use the treaty payment to make the Sioux rely on the government money. It wanted the time to teach the Sioux how to farm like white people did so they could survive without the buffalo. But the treaty fell apart when the government stopped paying and the Sioux continued to attack white settlers.

◀ Tepees were easy to move because the poles made a frame that could be loaded with cargo and dragged behind a dog or horse.

▶ Tepees were braced by long poles, with a smoke flap at the top to let smoke out. They were originally made of buffalo hide, but canvas was a much better material. By the 1860s, about half of all tepees were canvas.

◀ Native Americans camped in the area now covered by trees. Many lived here for years, working for and trading with the army. The local Sioux chiefs did not like the camp here because they thought their people had changed their way of life too much.

◀ For treaty talks, a big shelter was built using the poles and canvas coverings from tepees. Army and Native American men met, talked, and smoked a pipe to complete agreements they made.

Another treaty followed in 1868. The U.S. government promised more money, but the Sioux grew angrier as the army built more forts, and more settlers came through their lands. A Sioux chief named Red Cloud started Red Cloud's War, which lasted from 1866 to 1868. Fort Laramie had been one of Red Cloud's favorite trading posts, and it was left alone during the fighting. The war ended with a treaty that gave the Sioux their sacred hunting grounds and **reservation** land. But when gold was found in the **sacred** Black Hills in 1874, the treaty was broken by white **prospectors**.

When the army failed to keep white settlers and prospectors out of the Black Hills, President Ulysses S. Grant ordered all the Sioux onto reservations. The army attacked those who did not obey. Some Sioux, led by chiefs Sitting Bull and Crazy Horse, fought back. Fort Laramie soldiers played a big part in the Great Sioux Campaign of 1876. This was a series of battles that ended after the Sioux defeated Lt. Colonel George A. Custer's Seventh **Cavalry** at the Battle of Little Bighorn in 1876. However, the Sioux gave up their fight soon after and the army moved them onto **reservations**. After nearly 30 years of struggles, the Sioux had finally lost their traditional lands forever.

▶ The Sioux thought it was unhealthy to broil or roast meat. They cooked meat by boiling it inside buffalo stomachs. When they could trade for iron or tin cooking pots, cooking became much easier.

In 1837, many farming families in the United States couldn't make enough money from their farms. A **depression** in 1841 made things worse. These people started to think about moving west to begin new lives. Other people faced problems because of their religions. One group, called the **Mormons**, headed west and settled in Utah. Some people heard that gold was found in California. They went west hoping to get rich.

The first **pioneers** set out on the trail in 1841. In 1843, more than 1,000 pioneers made the five-month journey west. By 1867, more than 400,000 people had moved west, following one trail as far as the western edge of Wyoming, where they turned off on the Oregon, California, or Mormon Trails. More than 20,000 people died from accidents and **contagious diseases** on the journey. Although only about 400 pioneers were killed by Native Americans attacks, the fear of attack was great. After the difficult first part of the trip, when the pioneers learned how to work together and get used to the hard life on the road, they arrived at Fort Laramie.

For most of the year, Fort Laramie had few visitors. But during a 45-day period from early to mid-summer, up to 60,000 **emigrants** passed through the fort. In 1852, between 10,000 and 12,000 wagons carrying 50,000 to 60,000 emigrants arrived.

camp area

▲ At Fort Laramie, wagon trains camped across the river. Hundreds of camps set up at a time.

canvas cover   bow

axle   tongue

▲ Emigrants took their farm wagons and added stronger axles and wheels, plus a new tongue. They made bows to hold up a canvas cover. The wagons were small, about 4 by 10 feet (1.2 by 3 meters), and held 1,000 to 2,000 pounds (454 to 907 kilograms).

The emigrants were very busy during their stop at Fort Laramie. They bathed and washed their clothes. With the help of craftsmen at the fort, they repaired wheels, harnesses, and wagons. The emigrants bought flour, medicine, and other supplies from the fort trader. The stop allowed the emigrants to rest their animals or trade them for healthier animals.

Wagon trains then set off following guidebooks written by people who had made the journey or guides hired to help them find the best routes. Bad weather or changes in the land forced the pioneers to change the course of the trail. Emigrants talked with experienced guides at Fort Laramie about the best route west and what dangers to avoid. Some decided that the trip was too difficult and went back east. The rest went on their way, refreshed and ready to deal with the most difficult challenge ahead—crossing the Rocky Mountains!

► Emigrants ate simple meals of salt pork and camp bread. They slept outside the wagon, under it, or in a little tent.

▲ West of Register Cliff, emigrants passed over a low sandstone hill. Wagon wheels dug ruts into the soft stone. Today, ruts as deep as five feet (two meters) still exist.

▲ Register Cliff is eight miles (thirteen kilometers) west of Fort Laramie. Hundreds of emigrants carved their names into the sandstone as they passed.

A Soldier's Life

The **regiment** at Fort Laramie was made up of **companies** of **infantry** and **cavalry**. Each company had a barracks. The barracks, a long, two-story building, had a kitchen, **mess hall**, and day room downstairs. Upstairs, all the beds lined up against the two long walls, with hooks in the walls to hang clothes on and a trunk at the foot for belongings.

Behind the barracks were a series of **outhouses**. They were moved often, because the ground beneath them could not absorb any more waste. The fort's doctor complained about the health risks from these outhouses, but it took until 1886 for a big general **sink** to be built.

A soldier at Fort Laramie mostly lived a dull life of strict rules and routines. Most soldiers were recent **immigrants**, mainly Irish and German. Others joined because this was the only job they could find.

▼ The day room was used for meetings, repairing equipment, and keeping company records. This was a cavalry barracks, so it was also used for repairing saddles and bridles.

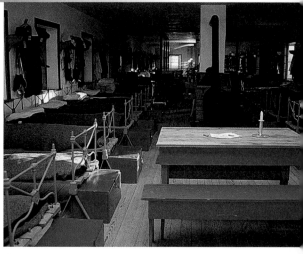

▲ This cavalry barracks was typical of barracks at Fort Laramie. Soldiers slept on straw mattresses, which they changed once a month.

water channel   hospital   cavalry barracks

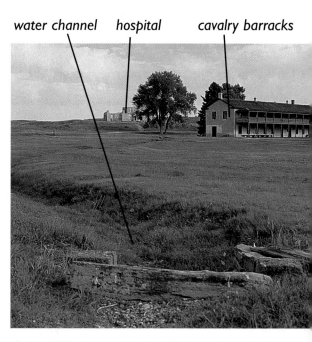

▲ In 1873, the twelve-bed hospital was built on a hill away from the rest of the buildings. Patients were usually treated by a soldier, not by a doctor. Only severe injuries, frostbite, broken bones, and high fevers sent a person into the hospital.

new guardhouse
general sink
old guardhouse

Many soldiers could not read or write and didn't understand that they had agreed to five years of hard work. Between 1865 and 1890, about one of every three soldiers at Fort Laramie deserted, or left without permission. Some were caught and punished, but many got away. Other soldiers liked it there, including one man who served at the fort for 37 years.

▲ The general sink was flushed by water flowing through the water channel near the parade ground and into pipes, then into the river.

Mostly, soldiers spent their days doing **drills** for five or six hours or **fatigue duty**, the army term for hard physical work, such as cutting wood, carrying water, or building houses. Soldiers rose at sunrise, worked all day with a break for a big lunch, and had some free time between their duties in the evening. At sunset, all soldiers and officers went to the parade ground, where the band played, the cannon fired, and the flag was lowered. Some soldiers had special duties, such as working for officers, baking bread, or teaching school. During free time, soldiers read, held dances, played music, had races, played games, and went fishing and hunting.

Sometimes soldiers received orders for field duty. This meant going on scout patrols away from the fort. They had 48 hours to prepare, then they marched out of the fort as the band played "The Girl I Left Behind Me." Before returning from the field, they cleaned up as best they could and marched back in. The band played "When Johnny Comes Marching Home."

▼ Soldiers generally hated guard duty. They worked a 24-hour shift, with 2 hours on and 2 hours off all day and night. They stayed fully dressed, and patrolled the grounds and prison.

cells

◄ The temperature could drop to −20° F (−29° C) in winter, and prisoners had only one blanket each and a wood stove to keep warm.

17

Officers at Fort Laramie

Officers were the elite, or the most respected, at Fort Laramie. Some went to college at **West Point** and were taught to be officers. Others earned their **commissions** in the field. Some were noncommissioned officers, or **NCOs.** They were chosen from the **enlisted** men, but they were ranked higher. Officers lived apart from the soldiers and were paid more than enlisted men, but they had to buy their own uniforms and equipment.

▶ An officer did paperwork on his field desk. Native American objects, like this lance, were highly prized. They were bought, traded for, or won in battle.

Officers spent much of their time doing paperwork. They had help from the NCOs, but they were responsible for all four of the different record books kept for each **company**. Each company had personnel records about the people in the company, a clothing book of army-issued equipment, a morning report book of daily tasks for each member of the company, and an order book of the company's commands.

Some officers moved their families to Fort Laramie with them. The army allowed 600 pounds (272 kilograms) of baggage and furniture for each officer, which is not a lot of furniture. So many families made simple furniture out of crates, borrowed furniture from the **regiment**, or bought items from families leaving the fort. An officer's field desk was thought to be necessary. The field desk and trunk always moved with the officer.

◀ The bachelor officers' bedroom in Old Bedlam is furnished to look like it did in 1853–1854. The furniture is very simple because it was made at the fort. It was normal for officers to sign their names on the walls before they moved out.

▶ This is a living room in Officers' Quarters B as it looked in 1872. The "sofa" is nothing more than cushions and fabric draped over crates.

There was never enough housing for officers at Fort Laramie. Bachelors lived in Old Bedlam, built in 1849. It was nicknamed after Bedlam, a mental hospital in England. Officers with families lived in one of the many houses around the parade ground. A junior officer had to move out of his house if a senior officer needed it. This was called **ranking out**, and it happened often. Some officers' families had to live in tents that they decorated as best they could.

◀ Many of the officers' quarters at Fort Laramie are in ruins today. Old Bedlam, at far right, is the oldest standing building in Wyoming.

▼ This big house was divided into two smaller living spaces. The left side is called Officers' Quarters B.

▲ This bedroom furniture was originally used at Fort Laramie.

Fort Laramie's Specialists

Some workers at Fort Laramie were assigned to the **regiment** and not to a **company**. The post surgeon was the doctor at the fort. He was usually a private doctor before he entered the army. The post surgeon diagnosed patients and prescribed medicines. The post surgeon's house had a study where he saw patients and kept a collection of animals and Native American items. He also kept records of the weather. His kitchen was used for surgery, since there was nowhere to do it at the hospital.

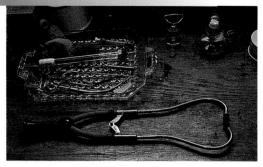

▲ The post surgeon used many of the same instruments that doctors use today, like stethoscopes, scissors, and sponges.

The chief post musician, the **chaplain**, and the quartermaster were all **NCOs.** The quartermaster was responsible for equipment and transportation, including the horses that pulled wagons. The biggest wagon fleet in the West was maintained by the quartermaster at Fort Laramie. He employed about 100 **civilians** in his shops and stables. These specialists kept the fort running, supplying goods and services to the regiment. Workers came from Denver, Omaha, and Cheyenne, and were paid with food, shelter, and $30 to $100 a month.

► The post surgeon collected animals to study.

The post trader was hired by the army, but worked for himself. He ran the store, post office, telegraph office, stagecoach, hotel, and bars. Native Americans were also hired by the army to act as scouts. Usually they were Pawnee, enemies of the Sioux. However, fights between between the scouts and the local Sioux were very rare. Other Native Americans, usually Sioux locals, were hired to care for the horses.

► NCOs lived in an apartment building near the hospital—now in ruins.

cavalry barracks

hospital

new bakery   old bakery   commissary   cavalry barracks

▲ The quartermaster kept his workers busy in this area with workshops and stables.

In 1802, the army first hired women to work as laundresses. Laundresses were the only women employed by the army. They were mostly poor, unmarried **immigrants** who wanted to see the West. There was one laundress for every 19 to 25 men. Laundresses were paid well, about $1 a month for each soldier, and $4 a month for each officer in her care. Soldiers were paid only $12 to $13 month. The laundresses also received housing, food, and fuel from the army. Many lived and worked across the river in an area known as Soapsuds Row. They often married **enlisted** men and NCOs.

▲ The post store, post office, telegraph office, and post trader's office were in the front building here. The building in back was added in 1883. It held the enlisted men's bar and the officers' club. The post trader was in charge of both buildings.

▼ The post store was built in 1849. Here is where soldiers, Native Americans, **prospectors, emigrants,** and families traded. Pottery jars, tin baths, candles, fabric, and plates were sold.

▼ Laundresses built tents on wooden platforms. They used wood fires to boil water for washing clothes and then hung wet clothes on the clothesline to dry.

21

Families at Fort Laramie

Even though married men were not allowed to join the army as **enlisted** soldiers, there were many families at Fort Laramie. Many soldiers fell in love with laundresses and received permission from their **company** commanders to marry.

Most enlisted soldiers' families lived across the river in tents made of canvas and wood. They decorated them carefully. The wives had all the normal chores of running a home, plus laundry to do if they were laundresses. Most laundresses didn't give up their careers when they married, partly because they earned more money than their husbands did. Their children went to school at the fort, taught by soldiers.

▲ Officers' dining rooms were furnished with fine china and silver.

Officers' families lived in houses mostly made from **lime grout**, unless they were unlucky and were **ranked out**. Most homes were too small, so some children often had to sleep in bedrooms created out of hallways. Wives decorated their homes with fancy table linens, plates, and silverware. They visited other wives on most days and entertained at home. They had some chores to do, but they usually hired a Native American woman or laundress to help around the house.

◄ **Outhouses** were very simple in design. Old newspaper was used for toilet paper and was hung on a nail in the wall.

outhouse   pump

◀ Officers' houses had small outhouses behind them. A water pipe ran from the water tower by the hospital to the officers' houses. Pumps drew water from this pipe. There was no running water inside, so people used a pitcher of water and a small tub in their bedrooms for washing.

Some wives brought servants from the East. Officers' wives were in charge of "civilizing" the fort. They organized dances, parties, and church services.

Some officers helped by starting a theater company. Officers' children were taught at home until they were old enough to go back east to school. Boys learned about the animals, landscape, and Native American culture around them. Girls learned how to act in society and entertain people.

Children wore clothes that looked like their parents' clothes. Boys even wore mini-uniforms. Children had great fun causing trouble, like braiding the tails of horses before dress parades, tying cans in dogs' tails and running them through dress parades, and throwing rotten eggs at buildings. However, many children got sick from diseases like measles, rheumatic fever, and brain fever.

▲ In 1877, twenty children between the ages of five and eleven went to school at the fort. School was held in the old bakery after the new one was built in 1883.

▼ Two boys shared this large room.

◀ Officers' children played with toys like this rocking horse and jigsaw puzzle.

23

Cooking and Eating

Anyone who worked for the army was fed by the army. The commissary, or cafeteria, stored food and gave out **rations.** Most of the food was brought into the fort. Each barracks had a kitchen where the **company's** food was cooked. There was also a central bakery, which baked all the bread for the fort. Soldiers traded their flour rations for loaves of bread.

The cooks and bakers were common soldiers, not trained cooks. This meant that the food wasn't very good most of the time. The cooks served bread and coffee for breakfast. Lunch was called "dinner," and it was the big meal of the day. On weekends, fresh meat was served, but on other days there was soup, stew, hash, coffee, and bread. For the evening meal, called "supper," cooks served bread and coffee with leftovers from dinner.

▲ Barracks' kitchens had very big cookstoves and tables on which to prepare food. The cook slept in a little room to the left of the stove.

Each of the officers' houses had its own kitchen. **Enlisted** soldiers served officers as cooks and housekeepers. These soldiers were called strikers. Strikers lived in the officer's house in a small room near the kitchen. Strikers were chosen because they were reliable.

▼ The barracks mess, or dining, hall held many men at once. They used sauces to flavor the food.

▲ Because the ovens were kept lit 24 hours a day, each day of the week, the bakers lived at the bakery. The bakery made up to 700 loaves of bread a day—even on Sundays.

Each company had a garden. The companies relied on their gardens for fresh fruit and vegetables, but food was hard to grow in the extreme climate.

Kitchens didn't change much during the 19th century. Food was baked inside a wood-burning stove and cooked on top of it as well. These stoves sometimes blew up. Cooks used ceramic crocks and jugs to make and store food in. Iron and tin pans held the food while it was cooking. People stored food in a pantry next to the kitchen.

The people at Fort Laramie used ice to cool food and drinks during the hot months. In winter, when the rivers were frozen, soldiers cut large blocks of ice from the rivers. They hauled them to ice houses along the riverbanks. Ice houses had limestone floors. The walls were sod or wood, also lined with limestone. About 150 tons of ice were cut and stored each winter at Fort Laramie. In summer, officers, soldiers, laundresses, the hospital, and the butcher shop received ice rations.

▲ Ice houses were by the river. They were lined in stone to help keep the ice cool. Most years, the ice lasted until July 4th, but some years it lasted until the end of September.

▶ This kitchen in Old Bedlam shows the kinds of mixing, storing, and baking utensils used. The pantry is to the left. The striker's bedroom is to the right.

▼ The oven doors are open on this cookstove. Kettles and pots were also put on top to heat.

▶ This icebox was used before people had refrigerators. A block of ice placed in one side kept food placed in the other side cool.

25

The Final Years

In late 1876, the Sioux gave up their fight for the Black Hills. At that point, all the Native Americans in the area served by Fort Laramie lived on **reservations**. Three years later, soldiers from the fort fought their last battle with Native Americans—this time with a group of Cheyenne who left their reservation. Once again, the purpose of Fort Laramie changed. Now it was used as a supply stop by gold **prospectors** heading for the Black Hills in present-day South Dakota. They used the fort as the pioneers had, resting, getting more supplies, and repairing their equipment. The soldiers were also given new duties. They worked to catch outlaws who robbed cargo wagons and stagecoaches.

By 1876, more than 1,000 people lived at Fort Laramie. About 660 were **enlisted** soldiers. Another 30 to 40 were officers. About 100 were **civilians** employed by the quartermaster to work in the workshops. The rest were wives, children, and laundresses. By the 1880s, the

▲ The birdbaths were added to the corners of the parade ground to make the fort feel more civilized.

parade ground was lined with trees on all sides and birdbaths at the corners. Sidewalks made from wood boards led between the houses along the parade ground and were lighted with gas lamps. There was even a sundial so people could set their watches. Raising cattle soon became the most important business in Wyoming. High beef prices made Cheyenne the richest town in the United States. The buffalo had been hunted off the plains, but cattle filled their places. The once wild **frontier** landscape was now tamed.

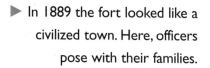

► In 1889 the fort looked like a civilized town. Here, officers pose with their families.

▲ Some of the buildings, like this administrative building, are still in ruins. But the old guardhouse, to the left, has been carefully restored.

Now that the West was settled, the army no longer needed a base at Fort Laramie. In 1886, the army decided to close Fort Laramie. The order to close came in 1889. In 1890, a **company** of African-American **cavalry** soldiers, or "Buffalo Soldiers," went to the fort and took apart most of the buildings. The 35,000 acres (14,000 hectares) the army had owned were opened up to settlers. The buildings were sold at a public auction. Some were lived in, and stayed in good shape. Left in the open air, with no one looking after them, many buildings fell apart over time.

▲ Ranchers used barbed wire fences to divide the once-open plains to raise cattle.

When the National Park Service took over Fort Laramie in 1938, it had much work to do. The most interesting and best-preserved buildings were **restored** carefully and furnished to look as they did in the 1800s. **Curators** found furniture and objects once used at Fort Laramie all over the country. Now, more than 100,000 people a year come to visit Fort Laramie to see this important place and to learn how it helped shape the future of the United States.

◀ Today, the commissary storehouse is used as a visitor center and offices for the park workers.

▶ The cavalry barracks day room is used to outfit school children who visit to learn about life at Fort Laramie. Children use the uniforms along the back wall to recreate a soldier's day.

Time Line

1803	President Jefferson completes the **Louisiana Purchase**
1804	Lewis and Clark set off on their expedition
1806	Lewis and Clark return to the East
1820s	First **mountain men** begin living in western hills
1834	Rocky Mountain Fur Company builds Fort William
1835	Fort William is sold to Fontenelle, Fitzpatrick & Company
1836	Fort William is sold to the American Fur Company
1837	First farming slump in United States
1841	Fort William is rebuilt using **adobe**, renamed Fort John but called Fort Laramie; second farming slump; first wagon train follows the Oregon Trail west
1849	United States government buys Fort Laramie
1851	First **treaty** is signed at Fort Laramie
1862	Original Fort John is demolished
1866-68	Red Cloud's War
1868	Second Native American treaty is signed
1869	**Transcontinental** Railroad is completed
1874	Gold found in the sacred Black Hills
1875	Army builds iron bridge over North Platte River
1876	Great Sioux Campaign to get whites out of the Black Hills
1876	Native American wars end shortly after Battle of Little Bighorn
1889	Army orders Fort Laramie to close
1890	Fort Laramie closed by army
1938	National Park Service takes over Fort Laramie

Site Map

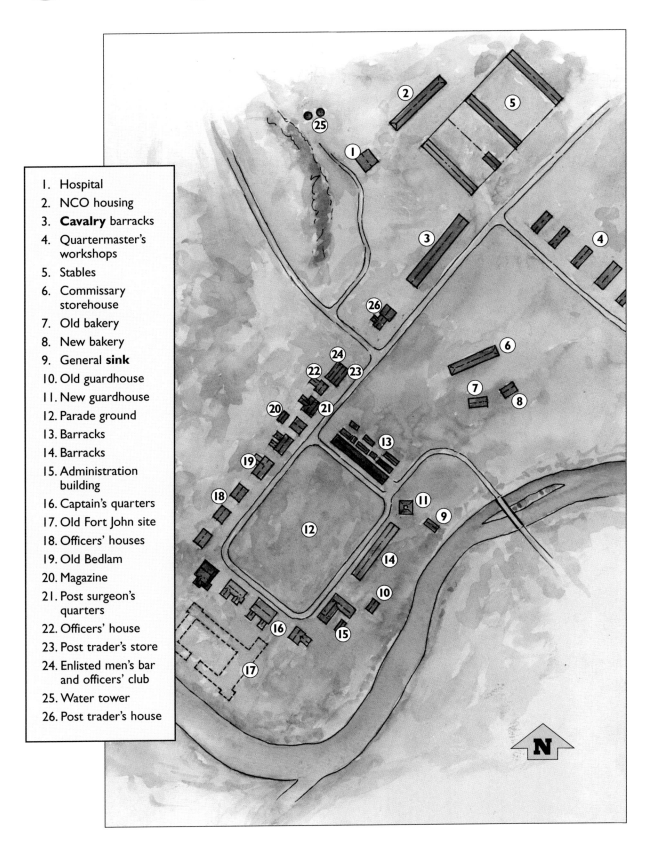

1. Hospital
2. NCO housing
3. **Cavalry** barracks
4. Quartermaster's workshops
5. Stables
6. Commissary storehouse
7. Old bakery
8. New bakery
9. General **sink**
10. Old guardhouse
11. New guardhouse
12. Parade ground
13. Barracks
14. Barracks
15. Administration building
16. Captain's quarters
17. Old Fort John site
18. Officers' houses
19. Old Bedlam
20. Magazine
21. Post surgeon's quarters
22. Officers' house
23. Post trader's store
24. Enlisted men's bar and officers' club
25. Water tower
26. Post trader's house

Glossary

adobe mixture of mud, straw, and a binder, such as horse manure

cavalry soldiers who travel and fight on horseback

chaplain Christian religious leader serving in the armed forces

civilian person who is not in the armed forces

commission paper that gives rank in the army

company unit of soldiers

contagious disease illness that can easily spread from person to person

curator person in charge of a museum

depression time when business is bad and many people lose their jobs

drill to learn a skill or process by doing it over and over

emigrant person who leaves one place to move to another place far away

enlisted person who has joined the army

fatigue duty physical work

frontier unsettled area that is next to a settled country

immigrant person who moves from one country to another to live

infantry soldiers who travel and fight on foot

lime grout a kind of concrete made from lime, used in blocks to build solid buildings

Louisiana Purchase land bought from France in 1803, stretching from the Mississippi River in the East to the Rocky Mountains in the West

mess hall military word for dining room

Mormon person belonging to the Church of Jesus Christ of Latter-day Saints

mountain man man living in the frontier, making a living trapping

NCO noncommissioned officer, an officer chosen from the enlisted men

negotiate to talk and bargain with others to reach an agreement

outhouse small building used as a toilet

pioneer person who goes somewhere or does something before others

Plains area of grassland in the middle of the Unites States, between the Mississippi River and the Rocky Mountains; also called the Great Plains

Pony Express mail delivery service that ran from St. Joseph, Missouri, to Sacramento, California, in 1860–1861. The route was 1,966 miles (3.164 km) long, and consisted of relays of young men—mostly teenagers—riding fast ponies or horses.

prospector person who searches for gold or other precious metals

rank out when a higher ranking officer took over the house of a junior officer

ration certain amount of something, especially food

regiment military unit made up of companies

reservation land given to Native Americans to live on, often far from their homeland, and often very different in geography

restored to make something look as it had at an earlier time

sacred religious idea, place, or item that a group of people respect greatly

sink large pool or pit used to hold waste or sewage

transcontinental across the continent; from the East Coast to the West Coast

treaty agreement between two or more countries or groups of people

Victorian having to do with the time when Queen Victoria ruled Great Britain, from 1837–1901

West Point college run by the U.S. Army where men and women are trained to be officers

*M*ore *Books* *to* *Read*

Eder, Jeanne M. *The Dakota Sioux.* New York: Raintree Steck-Vaughn, 2000.

Fox, Mary Virginia. *Women Who Shaped the West.* Danbury, Conn.: Children's Press, 1991.

Hewitt, Sally. *Plains People.* Danbury, Conn.: Children's Press, 1996.

O'Hara, Megan. *Frontier Fort: Fort Life on the Upper Mississippi.* Minnetonka, Minn.: Capstone Press, 1998.

Steele, Christy, ed. *A Covered Wagon Girl: The Diary of Sallie Hester, 1849-1850.* Minnetonka, Minn.: Capstone Press, 2000.

Stein, R. Conrad. *The Oregon Trail.* Danbury, Conn.: Children's Press, 1994.

Sundling, Charles. *Mountain Men of the Frontier.* Edina, Minn.: Abdo & Daughters, 2000.

Index